Flavours of a Sweet Rivalry

(Poetry and Motivation)

By

Christian Chidozie Okoro

COPYRIGHT

All rights reserved. No part of this book should be reproduced in any form without the due consent of the author.

Copyright:
Christian Chidozie Okoro
Chidospac Prints
© 2022

ISBN: 9798846519404
Imprint: Independently published

You can connect with the author on
Twitter: @chidospac
Instagram: @chidospac
Facebook: Christian Chidozie Okoro
Email: chidospac8@gmail.com

DEDICATION

This work of art is specially dedicated to all lovers of artistic football, to all true fans of Lionel Messi and Cristiano Ronaldo and to all lovers of poetry.

CONTENTS

Cover page
Title page
Copyright
Dedication
Contents
Preface
1) Cristiano Ronaldo
2) Lionel Messi
3) Sweet Rivalry
4) Over a Decade of Glory
5) The Longevity of Ronaldo
6) The Incontinence of Messi
7) The Hunger of Ronaldo
8) The Consistency of Messi
9) The Consistency of Ronaldo
10) The Passion of Ronaldo
11) Magic Wand of Messi
12) The Determination of Ronaldo
13) The Determination of Messi
14) The Hard Work of Ronaldo

15) The Focus of Messi
16) The Resilience of Ronaldo
17) The Accuracy of Messi
18) The Haughty Humility of Ronaldo
19) The Humility of Messi
20) The Wonder of Ronaldo
21) Team Work
22) Discipline
23) Love for Humanity
24) A Never Ending Debate

PREFACE

This book, titled "Flavours of a sweet rivalry" is designed to serve two definite purposes. The first is to celebrate the two outstanding players (Cristiano Ronaldo and Lionel Messi) who have tirelessly worked hard to place themselves on a level where they are considered as two of the greatest players who have graced the field of football.

The other purpose of this book is to inculcate into the readers the same mindsets that these two great individuals possess. If this second purpose is appropriately achieved, the readers of this book would find themselves successful in their respective fields.

The author of this book designed it in such an interesting way. This book is composed of about 24 unique poems and each of the poems has a theme of a great quality or attribute the author intends to teach or talk about. Messi and Ronaldo are the subject matters of each of those qualities. The poems depict the attribute in the players while the succeeding texts after the poems dwell more on how each attribute could be useful to any other individual in any other field.

The book comes handy for both football fans and individuals who are not really football fans. It is designed for everyone to enjoy it and as well learn from it.

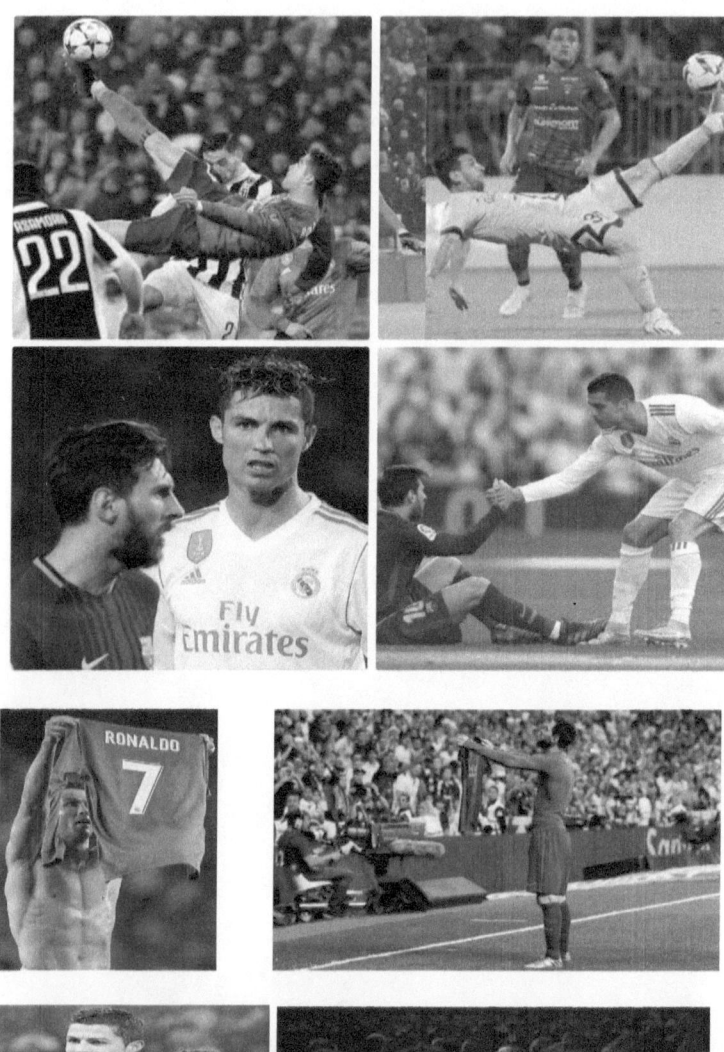

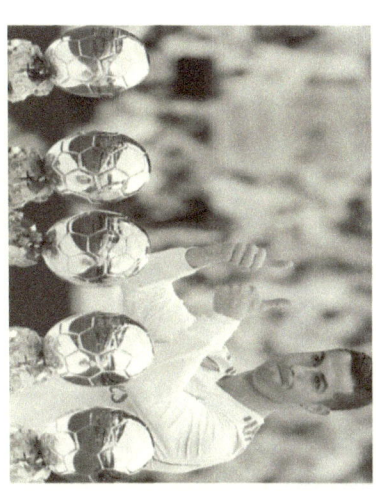
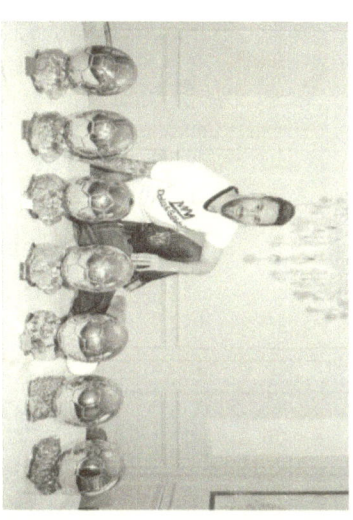
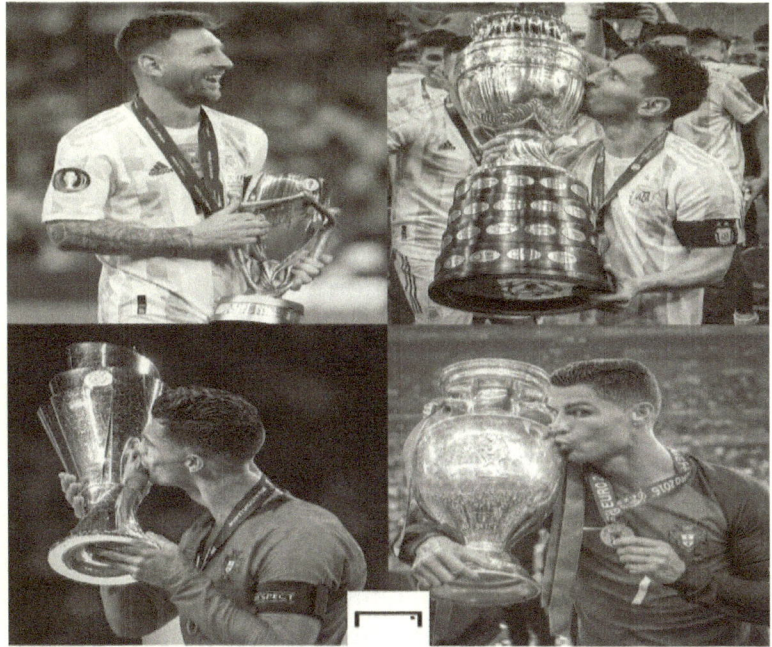

Flavours of a sweet rivalry

CRISTIANO RONALDO

It was a beautiful dawn
In Portugal, Madeira town
A young lad with tiny feet
Stepped on the green field
To walk through the path
Of grassy football kingdom

He did on the path walk
Today he wears a crown
And a dazzling red robe
Bearing the perfect number
Give it out to Cristiano Ronaldo
The one revered soccer king

He is the footballer poet
The rhyming of his feet
The rhythm in his steps
Create emotion of appreciation
In the minds of his audience

The assonance in his dribbling
The alliteration in his leg overs
Coupled with his hyperbolic shots
Create no euphemistic effect
To make it worse,
He coats this effect with his

Flavours of a sweet rivalry

Sarcastic celebrations
Give it out to Cristiano Ronaldo
The poetic and artistic baller

Though he runs-on lines
He strikes from all meters
His strikes create curves that glitter
Which make nets to shatter
His presence creates horror
Motions of his fast feet produce colours
He is the only banger of honours

His skyrocketing jumps defy gravity
His head speaks to nets with certainty
His heavily endowed feet are quick
No member of his feet is weak
His feet are fit to pull a trick,
Double trick and even a hat trick
Give it out to a banger of free kicks

Hope builder of his team
Show spoiler of the other team
The game changer of his time
The jinx breaker off his prime
Give it out to Cristiano Ronaldo
The one revered soccer King

The Flavour

The writer likens Cristiano's styles of play to poetry simply to depict how beautiful he makes his games appear. A popular saying goes thus; "whatever is worth doing is worth doing well". It is apparent that Cristiano Ronaldo understands this principle and the application of the principle in his football career has made millions of individuals fall in love with football.

Cristiano Ronaldo is such an influential player. Several football players get inspiration from his style of play. And several others seek to have in them his mentality. He is such a great athlete. Little wonder he is the most followed person on all social media outlets.

His huge fan base can simply be attributed to how artistic and beautiful he makes his games appear. People don't just love him because he possesses some facial and body beauty, they love him because he also incorporates some of his beauty into his game. He makes the game scintillating to watch. Cristiano pursues after excellence and perfection, and as a result Records and successes keep on chasing him.

What are the inferences?

If you must be successful in whatever you do, you must ensure that you don't just do what you do just for the sake of doing it. You must consciously put your mind into whatever you do. Try to incorporate arts into what you do so as to make it beautiful. This simply implies that you should do what you do skillfully. By putting conscious efforts to make your work beautiful, you would develop some elements of dedication to work in you. And true dedication is simply what you need to be the best or one of the best in your field.

Aim for perfection: From the poem you just read, it is very clear to see how Cristiano goes to any length just to play his game in the best possible fashion. All figures of speech used by the poet of the poem are used to point to the fact that Cristiano pays close attention to even the most insignificant aspect of his game to bring perfection into it.

When he puts out a beautiful play and scores a goal, he pulls out his unique celebration. Yes he alone is known for his celebration. It is his trademark celebration. When you put in enough beauty into the work of your hand, your effort would always make you stand out and you would be known for something which is uniquely yours, same way Ronaldo is known for his beautiful "siuuuuu celebration".

Several football players do "leg overs" however,

Flavours of a sweet rivalry

owing to how beautiful Ronaldo has made the skill appear, leg over is now almost like a Ronaldo's thing. Putting your best in what you do would make you stand out and it would make you to be sought for, as people would always be in need of your service.

From the poem, it can be read that Cristiano sometimes defies gravity while jumping to score a goal. Though the fact may be hyperbolic (exaggerated), but, that goes to tell you that for you to achieve any set goal in life, there are prices to pay. Good things don't come so easily, therefore you must be ready to always pay the requisite price to be great in what you do. Jumping to a high altitude to score a goal may appear beautiful to spectators but only the player knows the pains he takes. He alone knows the precautions he takes to have a safe landing so as to not fracture bones or dislocate the bones in the joints. This should also go the same way for you. You must put in that extra effort to see to it that your set goals in life are achieved. You should care less whether or not your efforts are commended. People's commendation or lack of commendation should not stop you.

Build yourself to a point that you would be so relevant and Indispensable in your work. We can actually speak of Ronaldo's importance in any team he plays in. He automatically becomes the tally's man of any team he finds himself in. This can simply be attributed to the fact that he puts his spirit into his game and the game has no option but to remain beautiful. Thus he becomes indispensable. Without him the team tends to lose. In order to be successful in your endeavor, you need to put in more skill and beauty into your work in such a way that you would become indispensable and irreplaceable in your field of work.

Flavours of a sweet rivalry

LIONEL MESSI

The Lion of the Argentinian clan
That incredible little man
Master in magical consistency
Baller Lionel Andres Messi

He's the defense mesmerizer
He pulls strong defensive pillars
He offers to men, brain teasers
As he, through their spaces meanders

His eyes are like the eagles'
His feet hit targets when they kick
His body is just for the dribbles
His kicks wears him a hat trick

His two feet are so fortified
His left foot leave men terrified
His motions leave fans electrified
His identity has already been verified

While mates relinquish, he still persists
When they're selfish, he still assists
He scores a hattrick with great tactics
And graces braces, oh! What a film trick!

Flavours of a sweet rivalry

The king of the football kingdom
Executive of the soccer corridor
The bagger of the coveted Ballon d'or
He is never satisfied with more

Like the lion he is, He's tireless
He's calm, brave and fierce
On the box he is so ruthless
As he runs in with energetic pace

He made it rain in Spain
Causing to many pain
Bringing to Barca gains
Now he explores another chance
In the Paris city of France

He is a Lion, he's not a cub
Lionel outscores a club
Scoring daily with forward gear
91 beautiful goals in a year

He's not just a record maker
The Lion is a record breaker
He is not just a play maker
He's a wonderful way maker
And a graceful goal scorer

Flavours of a sweet rivalry

The Flavour
The flavour we can derive from this poem is accepting your uniqueness. The poet begins the poem by making mention of the physical stature of Lionel Messi. Well, Messi cannot be termed a very short man, however he does not have the same height as most football players. But does his size pose any challenge to his game? Not all. In fact, he has over the years used his size and stature to improve his styles of play.

In the poem above, the poet mentions how he mesmerizes defenders with his dribbles as well as meandering in and out of their spaces. The truth is that everything about Messi's style of play is so unique. He incorporates uniqueness in his game.

If you watch Messi play, the ball is hardly collected from his feet. He does what he pleases with the ball whenever the ball is in his possession. Little wonder he is always bagging trophies and awards to his credit.

Winning seven Ballon d'or awards is no mean feat in football, it takes a person who is committed and consistent in his craft to achieve such a great honour.

Now what are the inferences?
Try to identify your strengths and dare to continuously and consistently put your strengths into

use. There is something that makes you stand out from the crowd. Try to fully identify it and don't relent in giving your best to it so as to improve in what you do. The thing that can make you stand out may be so little, it may not be such a big deal. You just have to identify that little thing you are sure that you can do. You must not be the best at it, but by constantly doing it, you would find yourself improving at it.

Always try to attach uniqueness in whatever you do. Let there be something about the way you do things that would make people always link you to what you do. Add a touch of beauty to your works so that it would stand out from the work of others.

Learn how to creatively use your uniqueness to your advantage. There are reasons why you possess those features. One of the reasons is for you to stand out and be distinct from every other individual, another reason is for you to utilize that uniqueness in you to be outstanding. For these reasons, always think about doing or creating something no one has ever done before. By doing so, your success and breakthrough in your field will not be negotiable.

Let's bring Lionel Messi into this one more time, we can all agree that his style of play is unique to him alone, no other player plays just like him, even though speculations have it that he plays like the late Argentinian hero, Diego Maradona. Well, the playing style of Maradona might have had some effects on Messi. However Messi created a playing style that is uniquely his. The way he holds the ball in his feet, the way he dribbles, the way he takes defenders unawares to score and all his unique playing styles are products borne out of his uniqueness.

The lesson here is to identify what makes you unique and put it into use for your advantage. Learn to convert what appears as a weakness into your strength. Always think of being the best at what you do. And if you stay true to all these, just like Lionel Messi, you too can become a super star.

Flavours of a sweet rivalry

SWEET RIVALRY

The crowning of Kaka a king
Offered to the football community
Yet another two contentious kings
Cristiano Ronaldo and Lionel Messi
This contention excites the community

A new king emerges a year down the lane
The king was Cristiano Ronaldo
He emerged to rule alongside the queen
In the Manchester axis of England
The year after in the Catalan city of Spain
Came an overthrow of the king in England
The new King Messi, came only to win

This new king from Spain
Enjoyed a four year uninterrupted reign
Giving the football community reasons
to scream
Giving the dethroned king more reasons
to dream

In a year he achieved up to 91 goals
A feat not achieved by any other king
Following the year of twenty-twelve
His choicest rival banged 69 goals
The two kings focus to honour, bring

Following the year of twenty-twelve
There was a well designed coup
To take out King Messi from the throne
The coup was successfully plotted
By the dethroned King Ronaldo
To reclaim his throne and have a second reign

The four to one thrashing by his rival
Was later compressed to four to three
The football community truly obtained
Joyful moments from the battle in Spain

Following the sarcastic goal celebration
Of showing his Barca shirt
to the community of Santiago Bernabeu
A year after the Camp Nou community
Received the same treat of seeing
The number 7 blue shirt of CR7

The two rival kings eventually got tied
At five to five reigning years
Though the shorter king acquired
a perfect number of reigning years
But the battle and rivalry line
Has only just been drawn

The Flavour
One sure way to grow and improve in every field or endeavor is by taking challenges. And this is

Flavours of a sweet rivalry

something these two fantastic individuals have done over the years and keep doing even till tomorrow. They have used their rivalry to push each other to a point that they are arguably regarded as the best players that have ever graced the field of play.

Ronaldo does not want to settle for less, he wants to be known as the best. Therefore he does everything possible to outplay Messi who stands as a contender to him, or at least the closest contender, in terms of quality of play

Same goes for Lionel Messi, deep inside of him, he sees himself as the best and he does not want anybody to outplay him, not even his closest contender, Cristiano Ronaldo in terms of quality of play. This challenge between them creates a fierce rivalry between. But it is called a "Sweet Rivalry" because they also benefit from the effects of the rivalry. In fact, the fans too are entertained by the effects of the rivalry. The fans have been the ones who have made the game of soccer very interesting for the past two or more decades, and still counting. You definitely cannot imagine what soccer would have been like, if there were no Messi and Ronaldo. You also cannot say with certainty that if this sweet rivalry never existed between the both of them, they would have had the numbers of Ballon d'or awards that they have. No, that wouldn't have been possible.

The sweet rivalry was so vital to their careers. You can remember that at some point in the year 2012, Messi had four Ballon d'or awards, while Ronaldo had only one. You can imagine how Ronaldo would have been feeling seeing Messi clinch the highly coveted award from 2009 to 2012, consecutively. It must not have been a good feeling for Ronaldo. At least because of the rivalry. Well, the rivalry between them created motivation and determination in him. He kept on pushing harder and luckily, he clinched the award in 2013. And to prove what the award meant to him at that point in time, he emotionally broke down in tears, while giving his appreciation speech on the stage. Those tears must have meant; "Messi, after stressing my life for four consecutive years, I'm using this Ballon d'or to shame you"

What are the Inferences?
A healthy growth can only come from a healthy competition. Now who should you compete with? Compete with the best, but ensure that it is a healthy competition. It should not be the type of competition that would make you envy your competitor and want to run him or her down. The competition between Messi and Ronaldo is very healthy, though the fans make it look unhealthy, but thank goodness, fans are

far away from the football pitch.

Having the best as your competitor, creates in you, the determination to match his or her level. Now, when you are determined to be as good as the best, even though you don't eventually become as good as the best, you would experience a great deal of improvement in the process of trying to be as good as the best.

Having the best as your competitor is another good way of pushing yourself harder, as it creates motivation in you. It creates in you the motivation to never want to settle for less. It does to you what it does to Messi and Ronaldo. For each of them, the hidden motive behind the records they create and break is to be named as the greatest of all times (GOAT), each of them wants to be better than the other.

So when you have it in your mind to be better than the best in your field, if you continue to go harder and not relent, you may get to the level where you would also be regarded as one of the best heads in the field.

Having the best as your competitor, gives the people something to talk about. Now when you become a subject of discussion in the lips of other people, you may not want to live below their expectations, and that quest of wanting to live up to their expectations, would definitely push you to be very good at what you do.

Learn to always take challenges from people, though in a healthy way. Don't let rivalry create envy in you, that may make you want to undo someone else. A little bit of jealousy that can push you is fine. Use the best as a standard of measurement, but strive to always be better than you were yesterday.

Flavours of a sweet rivalry

OVER A DECADE OF GLORY

There arose two writers
One from Madeira Portugal
The other from Argentina
They write beautiful stories
Stories of wondrous glories

Other writers are overshadowed
By the writers, Messi and Ronaldo
They've written and rewritten history
For the fluid of their inks overflow
They've had over a decade of glory

These writers also are rulers
Like dictators they refuse to abdicate
They want to rule forever
Their leadership no one should replicate

Being the best seems like a birthright
They grab the Ballon d'or like it's theirs
Every year they continue in their fight
To retain their kingly throne and palace

Apart from others, they dwell on high
Though they come down to play with them
But forget not to retain their lofty heights
They see themselves as rare gems

Give it out to Lionel Andres Messi
Who never mediocrity sees
A great rewriter of the soccer story

The creator and breaker of history
Cheers to his several years of glory

Give it out to Cristiano Ronaldo
The king who a lot of things knows
The one jinx breaker in history
The writer of new football stories
Cheers to his several years of glory

The Flavour

The longevity of Messi and Ronaldo can be easily attributed to their habits of not letting their achievements get into their heads. These two amazing footballers have practically achieved almost everything in their fields, but when you see them play, they play as though they are playing for the very first time. This is why beautiful records keep chasing them. They give out their best in order to move past the average level, because to them, mediocrity is an abomination.

Messi and Ronaldo never feel complacent because of their achievements. Even with all the records they have over the years, created and broken, they still train as hard as other players, if not harder. They still feel hungry to achieve, little wonder their age is not a limiting factor to them.

What are the inferences?
As long as you still breathe, keep achieving. There is always more to achieve. There is no limit to what you can achieve. Keep knocking on those doors. Never get tired. And never create a room for complacency. Complacency is a feeling of self satisfaction for your achievements. When this feeling sets in, it gives you reasons to believe that you have arrived and you consequently have no need to keep working hard. Now, when you allow complacency to take over you, you may be unaware of the time you would begin to lose your glory. You may be enjoying the old glory but that can only keep you at a place, ensuring that you are not improving.

If anyone should feel relaxed because of his achievements, that person should be Messi or Ronaldo. The number of goals each of these guys scores in a year may be the total career goals of another player. But does this get into their heads? Not really! They still work harder as though they have not even achieved anything. This is the mind that you need to have a long reign in your field.

In whatever you do, have it as one of your major plans to create your own story. Try to leave your

Flavours of a sweet rivalry

marks on the sands of time. Nobody would ever forget Messi or Ronaldo, not even the tenth future generation to come. It is not a mean feat for two players to collectively win up to twelve Ballon d'or awards, up to ten European golden shoe awards, up to nine Champions league titles, and other numerous beautiful achievements.

Have in your plans to do something that would make you never to be forgotten. Dare to also have several years of glory

Flavours of a sweet rivalry

THE LONGEVITY OF CRISTIANO

The ageless warrior
Age is but a number
As the days get older
This warrior gets stronger
Yes he gets also younger
He's the past, present and future

His mates are now so serious
So serious with life
They're off the pitch strife
Chilling with friends and wives
He still plays to bag honours

Boys who once called him "Sir"
Now call him "Mate"
He still keeps his weight
Still bags enviable rates
The warrior is always on fire

When mates ponder to retire
He counts on how many years more
He's not scared to knock on the doors
Built in England, Spain, Italy or
Back to the door in Manchester area

Give it out to the ageless warrior
The conqueror of territories

> The one who charges like batteries
> Just to cross all blocked boundaries
> Give it out to the glutton for honours

The Flavour

Now tell me, do you find it surprising to hear that Cristiano is the only player from the Manchester United squad that won the 2008 UEFA Champions league against Chelsea, that is actively playing football in Europe now. Every other player in that squad has either retired from actively playing in Europe or has completely hung his boots. So why is Cristiano still playing? Was he the youngest in that Manchester United squad? I don't think he was the youngest. At least, I am sure that from the ages we know, Wayne Rooney is a year younger than Cristiano Ronaldo. But today, Wayne Rooney is a manager, while Cristiano still plays actively in Europe. Players who were very tiny when he was playing as a young youth are today playing with him as teammates.

Cristiano Ronaldo has been very consistent for close to two decades now. He has been winning trophies and personal awards and he keeps doing so even till tomorrow. He does not even put his age into consideration. To him, age is just but a number. When he trains, he trains like a 20 year old youth, even though he is approaching the age of 40. In fact, he joined Juventus from Real Madrid in the year 2018, when he was 33 years old. After carrying out some medical tests on him to determine his fitness, the medical team of Juventus reported that the 33 years old man possessed the fitness of a 20 year old youth. That sounds amazing, right? Well it didn't just happen by chance. It is from years of hard and diligent work. He is such a disciplined player who applies discipline in keeping fit and conditioning his body and mind so as to keep playing on a high level.

Most African players, especially in my country Nigeria, when a player gets to age 35, they believe that it is time to retire. It's such a shame. People are supposed to retire when they can no longer play with strength. But the reverse is the case among some of my African brothers. I don't want to mention names, but there are some Nigerian exceptional players that I still desperately want to hear the reason behind their retirement.

Cristiano Ronaldo is approaching the age of 40, and he does not look like someone who's retiring soon.

What are the inferences?
Age is but a number. And the longer you perform in a particular field, the better you get, as experience has

always been known to be the best teacher. Jumping from one boat to another or stopping half way when you start can never make you the best in your field. Mention all the individuals who are considered as the best, apart from the ones whose days were cut short by death (Examples; Michael Jackson, Tupac, Bob Marley, and footballers who died in their prime), no other person became the greatest by starting and stopping half way. So that exceptional Nigerian footballer whom I choose not to mention his name, if he had allowed his career to last for more years, he would have been in the debate of who the world's GOAT is.

In whatever you do, try to remain in it for a good number of time, that way you would make yourself a master in it. But as soon as you jump to another field, you would start anew to learn about the activities in that new field, and the sad fact is that the time that you would use to learn about the new field could also be used to make yourself a master in the initial field.

So in whatever you do, dare not to see your several years of service as reasons to want to retire tomorrow. If possible, keep doing what you are doing until you are not able to do it again. It still boils down to passion. Dare to love what you do, so that you cannot easily let go. And the truth is that if you cannot easily let go of what you do, and hold tenaciously to it, the chances of excelling through it are high. Experience would always beat a skill acquired from an immediate training.

Flavours of a sweet rivalry

THE INCONTINENCE OF MESSI

He eats using his feet
And not using his teeth
He feeds on the goals
As he pushes in the ball
To the back of nets

The more goals he gets
The more he wants to eat
The more goals he eats
The more he is unsatisfied

Cabinet full of trophies
And awards he has
He needs a cabinet like a city
Bigger than Cabinets in his house
To store more awards and trophies

His needs are always met
But his needs are never met
As he needs to just do all
He is never satisfied with more

He is truly the go getter
Just like the heavy eaters
Whose bellies are expandable
Lionel has this incontinence
Which makes him dependable

The Flavour

Lionel Messi is a very hungry player. Little wonder his greatness keeps on flourishing on a daily basis. Apart from not winning the World cup yet, Lionel Messi has won practically almost every trophy there is to win in football. But is he satisfied with all the wins? Hmm.. He may be happy with his achievements but he is not satisfied with them and this explains why he is always gunning for more.

He appeared in the Copa America final for up to four times, he lost the first three finals, oh! How sad!!! In fact, his frustration was visibly seen in the third final that Argentina bottled against Chile. Messi unfortunately lost a penalty shoot out, which was one of the contributory factors to why Argentina didn't win that final. His frustration was seen as he cried sore. He even attempted to call it a quit as regards playing international football, though he later reconsidered his stance on quitting.

But the flavour from Messi's hunger to always take Argentina to finals is that he is very hungry for success. And It takes a man who desires to achieve greatness to feel downcasted and disappointed when he is not succeeding as desired.

Now, despite all his achievements, Messi continues to

work hard to achieve it all. We saw how he took Argentina to the World cup final in 2014 where they battled against Germany. If not that luck resided more in the camp of the Germans, Messi would have won his first World cup in 2014. His hunger is the reason why he still takes his country to the World cup tournament.

Currently, he has won seven Ballon d'or awards (the highest number won by a single player in history) Now the question is; Why is he still eager to feature in every game? Why was he sad when his coach in PSG substituted him for another player? What else is he still playing for after winning seven Ballon d'or awards? Why does he still want to score goals despite the big numbers of goals he has scored?

Well, there is only one answer to the above questions. And the answer is that Lionel is a hungry and incontinent player. He is never satisfied with all his numerous and beautiful achievements. He has put out several magics in the way he dribbles and the way he scores, yet he is still evolving everyday.

What are the inferences?
No matter how much, too much is never enough. Look out for the world's richest men, they are rich in billion dollars, not just million dollars. If any of them is asked to stop acquiring wealth and depend only on

what they have acquired, they would have sufficient and even surplus after they must have used the money to fend for themselves even to their sixth generations. Wow! What is surprising is the fact that one man owns these billion dollars.

Now the question is; If a man like Elon Musk, Jeff Bezos or Bill Gate, after making his first one million dollars, took a relaxation or a complacency pill to chill, giving himself accolades that he had achieved greatly by acquiring a whooping sum of one million dollars, would he be in the list of the world top richest men? The answer is No.

Another thing is that even though these richest men are at the level where they are, they still work hard everyday to increase their net worths, which is exactly what Messi does, but in the world of football.

And if you must be successful in your own field, you must have those elements of discontentment and dissatisfaction for what you think you have acquired. Always see yourself as though you are empty and you need to be filled up. Always Compare your achievements with the achievements of the best in your field and track your success through such comparisons. Don't be content with your achievements if there are more to achieve. Go for more.

Flavours of a sweet rivalry

THE HUNGER OF RONALDO

The more food he takes in
The more hungry he gets
The more goals he scores
The more he seeks for the net

A thousand miles already covered
Few other miles yet to be covered
But too much isn't just enough
For with the game he is so in love

Tested, tried and trusted
Moving from England to Spain
In Italy too, he was tested
But the result was so much gain
Now he is back to England
To feed again from the land

He is the insatiable warrior
Never satisfied with records
He eats all foods and Oreos
And he after asks for more
Just like his gastrin,
he has elastic feet
He is the eater who never sits

He is a true glutton for fame
Does all he could to keep his name

Flavours of a sweet rivalry

> Everyday he dares no to be same
> He works not to acquire shame
> Always feeding on a higher realm

The Flavour

To succeed in life, you must desire to succeed. The powerful word here is "DESIRE". Desire comes in the form of hunger. All successful people feel hungry for success. They are never satisfied with their achievements, they are always seeking to achieve more.

Cristiano is a perfect example in this case. Despite the fact that he has practically achieved almost everything there is to achieve in football, he still plays as a newcomer who is seeking to be famous. Despite the number of goals he has scored in his career, he still seeks to score some more.

His hunger can be visibly seen in his frustration on the pitch, when he is not scoring or winning. This frustration sometimes makes him appear arrogant or rude, however the arrogance or rudeness can simply be attributed to his hunger to always win the game.

A number of strikers can be comfortable when they have in their entire career the number of goals Cristiano scores within three years, but this hungry player known as Cristiano Ronaldo never gets satisfied with his number of goals, even though he outscores a club.

What are the inferences?
It has been mentioned above that one of the factors that can easily make you fall or fail in your journey is complacency. Whenever you start letting your little achievement in your field get into your head, that little achievement would in turn give you no good reason to work hard and to be better at what you do. And when you fail to work harder to improve yourself, the consequence is simply that you would hardly amount to greatness in your field.

Now the right thing to do is to leave all past records in the past, and focus on every new day to create something new for yourself.

Dare to feel hungry for success the same way you feel hungry for food. When a person feels hungry for food, what does the person do? I guess the person looks for a way to get something to eat in order to satisfy his hunger for food. Same thing goes in this game of achieving success, you need to have this burning desire to succeed and you shouldn't feel comfortable when you are not achieving what you desire. When this hunger to succeed is successfully created in you, you would be configured in a way that you would

Flavours of a sweet rivalry

want to quench the hunger. Now, in this configuration, you would get to find out in what areas you need to work hard in order to succeed.

One sure way to have the hunger to succeed is by falling in love with what you do. Now let's take it back to the food analogy. You naturally find yourself wanting to have more of your favorite food simply because of the love you have for the food. In the same way, if you can fall in love with what you do, you would also see yourself wanting to get the very best out of what you do. You would always devote your time and energy to it to see that you become the very best at it.

It has been stressed enough that all you need to succeed in whatever you do is passion.
The passion for what you do is what actually creates that desire to succeed.

Cristiano's passion is unquestionable, he loves the game so much. If you can possibly dig deep into his heart, you would definitely discover that his heartbeat is to win every trophy and award that can possibly be won in football. No other man would have such a mindset than a man who is always hungry to achieve greatness in every circle. How do we even know that he has a mind to succeed in his game? It is obvious to see, at least for the fact that in each game he plays, he is either breaking a standing record or creating a new record. He speaks on several occasions that; "He does not chase after records but records chase after him" Those words must always come from a mind that is always desirous and hungry for success. And that explains why he is a success. For you to also be a success, you need to have the same mindset as Cristiano.

Flavours of a sweet rivalry

THE CONSISTENCY OF RONALDO

The ageless young man
The youngest old man
The strongest old man

Age to him is but a number
His feet give always a banger

Skillful abilities remain the same
He everyday lives up to his name
He is the very maestro of his game
Respect to the king of the soccer realm

His abilities are daily renewed
He never rests until he pays his dues
He only relaxes when he screams "Siuu!!!"
Respect to the one who ages with clues

His beautiful and alluring leg overs
Seem to be living on pitches forever
His great speed like a running cheetah
Tend to increase as he gets older

His name shall be written with gold
With fonts not faint but very bold
For as he grows daily old and bold
His skills acquire more beautiful molds

Flavours of a sweet rivalry

The Flavour

Winners never quit and those who easily quit, hardly win. In the journey through the path of success, irrespective of how many times you try and fail, quitting on the way is what truly makes you a failure but consistency in trying until you get it right would certainly make you successful in your endeavor.

Cristiano Ronaldo is the perfect case study as regards the issue of consistency, This fantastic player never stops knocking on the door until the door is opened. We all know Cristiano Ronaldo as a good footballer and a fantastic goal scorer, however in his goal scoring prowess, he tried several times to score a goal using the bicycle kick skill, but most of the times, the luck was not always on his side. The one or two goals he scored using that skill were not as beautiful as he wanted them to be. But did that discourage him from trying? No, not at all. He kept on trying. And that continuity in trying is what we refer to as "consistency".

A person who is consistent at trying is bound to get it right someday. And one beautiful thing about consistency in trying is that the more you keep trying, the better you get and the more you improve at what you do. Show me any other player who can score a bicycle kick goal which can be as beautiful as the one Ronaldo scored against Juventus in the

Flavours of a sweet rivalry

Champions league elimination stage in 2018, the beauty of the goal made the fans of the team he was against to applaud him. The truth is that the constant attempts he had to score such a goal gave him more precision and as he improved, he was able to score that beautiful goal.

It is also his consistency in dribbling using leg overs that gives him the trademark of the player who owns the leg over style of dribbling. Ronaldo is so consistent in everything he does. His trademark celebration after scoring a goal cannot be overemphasized. In fact, due to the beauty in the celebration, most football players sometimes celebrate using Ronaldo's "siuuuu celebration" when they score, but that may not have been happening if he wasn't consistent with the celebration. Consistency has made Ronaldo appear as though he is even bigger than the game of football itself.

What are the inferences?
No lasting success is achieved by starting and stopping. When you always start and stop without completing the things you start, you will end up being a jack of all trades and a master of none.

Learn this beautiful attitude of consistency. Whatever good strategy that you have, keep on putting it into a good use. As long as the strategy has once yielded a good result, when you apply the same strategy over and over again, it will continue to yield good results. Don't worry about getting it all at a moment. It is a gradual journey, you will surely get there if you do not give up on the way.

Consistency also creates commitment. Yeah, when you have your mind at doing something repeatedly in order to actually get it right, you would unconsciously get into what you do, getting into what you do is synonymous to being committed to what you do. And through commitment, your success is not negotiable.

When you try and fail or when you try and get some undesired results, you can feel bad for your bad result, but don't let your bad result keep you down, instead take all the energy that emanate from the bad feeling of your bad result and invest the energy into your energy store to try again. As you try again, resolve within you that your new outcome can never be as the previous one, this way, your success is guaranteed.

Let's relate what we just stated with Ronaldo's Ballon d'or journey with Lionel Messi. Ronaldo was the first to win the award in 2008. Now for the next four

Flavours of a sweet rivalry

consecutive years, Messi won the award four good times. Well, in all these times, Ronaldo was one of his closest contenders. Oh! How would Ronaldo be feeling for failing to clinch what he so desired to win in those years.

Ordinarily, it would be easy for a person who easily quits to give up putting in hard work, since the hard work was not producing the desired result? But did he stop trying? No he did not. He even put in more hard work to achieve his goals of being the best player in the world. Did his hard work pay off? Of course, hard work would always pay off. He went ahead to win the highly coveted award two years in a row, bringing the score between himself and his rival, Leo to 4 to 3 in favor of Lionel Messi. Messi went on to win the award the following year bringing the score to 5 to 3 in favor of Messi. Well, Relentless Ronaldo does not know how to give up. He went on to win the award for the next consecutive two years. Oh what a decade of beautiful rivalry between the two kings of football. Kudos to Messi for adding two more Ballon d'or awards to his cabinet. We are watchful of the magic that Ronaldo's consistency would perform again.

To be successful in whatever you do, dare to learn from Ronaldo's consistency, for winners never quit and quitters never win.

Flavours of a sweet rivalry

THE CONSISTENCY OF MESSI

King of magical Consistency
King Lionel Andres Messi
The king who shows no mercy
Though his last name is Messi
He makes opponents' game, messy

Ninety one beautiful goals in a year
Did his scoring motion stop?
No, he still applies scoring gear
Winnings awards, honours and cups

A record breaker not a chaser
The records run to and after him
He's the way breaker and maker
Defenses collapse just for him

His styles everyday are evergreen
His burning desire is to often win
When other mates opt to retire
The Lion still plays on fire

His accuracy sure is like clockwork
As the lion ages
He gets as strong as a rock
Fair to call him a rock of ages

Flavours of a sweet rivalry

> He stands before giants so brave
> He rather keeps his face unshaved
> Than to hide his face in a cave
> Big ups to the lion who wins and waves

The Flavour

Yes, it is true that Cristiano Ronaldo is a very consistent player, but Ronaldo's consistency might have also been propelled by threats posed by another consistent player, Lionel Messi. The ability to win four Ballon d'or awards four years in a row (2009-2012), winning the award again in 2015 and bringing up the number of wins to the perfect number 7, can only be achieved by another very consistent player.

Messi's consistency is actually mind blowing. We can still recall the wonder of scoring 91 goals in a calendar year. It takes a person who never gives up on the way, to achieve such a wonderful feat. Messi and Ronaldo have a way of making great feats appear so easy because of the beauty of the feats.

Great achievers repeat a good strategy over and over to maintain the good result they obtain. While maintaining the working strategy, they also create rooms for improvement. It was a contribution of Messi's consistency to the team, Barcelona that made the team to win the La liga trophy year in year out

Flavours of a sweet rivalry

(The efforts of other players are respected and recognized too). Messi is a gentle natured person, but deep inside of him, he knows how to put a working strategy into use to achieve the results he wants and he does this repeatedly. This is why he keeps achieving the great feats he achieves in the game of football.

What are the inferences?
Be intentional about every step you take. Be like Messi who understands the principles of success and tends to apply them consistently.

Be about what you do in your mind. You must not show your strategy to people, or you must not let them know that you know or what you do. Just keep on doing what you know and let them see your good results. Messi is good in this field, which is also why he appears more humble than Ronaldo. However one good thing about Ronaldo is that his achievements also match his seemingly showy attitude. In this case, just know yourself and live out your best life. The idea is to be consistent at doing what works for you.

Don't let your enormous result affect your consistency and commitment. Some people easily lose the drive to keep on working hard when they achieve greatly. Truth is; in the year 2012, Messi had every reason to feel so relaxed after scoring his first 60 goals, because scoring up to 60 goals in a year is such a great feat for a great player. But was his consistency affected? No, not at all. He went ahead to score a whopping number of 91 goals, perhaps his target might have been to score up to a hundred goals in that year.

Do not stop or relent when your achievements seem to be very good. That should even give you reasons to work harder, so that you don't fall off from the high level that you have successfully mounted upon. Messi currently has 7 Ballon d'ors and over 700 goals heading to a thousand goals. But is he still aiming to win more trophies and awards? Is he still desirous to score goals? The answer to the above questions is YES.

Now if Lionel Messi, with all his achievements in his career, still puts in consistency to achieve more and more wonderful results, then you need to be intentional in applying consistency in whatever you do, for through consistency, the achievements of wonderful results would be absolutely guaranteed.

THE PASSION OF RONALDO

The smell of the green grass
Is my daily motivation
To remain in the topmost class
My prioritized preoccupation
For deeply rooted is this passion

The view of the true or false fans
A cause to meet expectations
So we must score by head or hands
We must respect their emotions

The fluid flowing through the vein
Is the fuel that gives feet motions
We must run ignoring the pain
We must gain in all competitions

Though we fall here and there
We rise, we pick up the pieces
We press on until we get there
For the love at last, suffices

Deeply rooted is this passion
In smiling sun or weeping rain
loss or win, our team is our nation
We shall share in her joy or pain

Flavours of a sweet rivalry

> In smiling sun or in weeping rain
> I simply cannot feign
> My intense love for this game
> The awesome and beautiful game

The Flavour

For you to be successful in whatever you do in life, you must have a strong passion for what you do the same way Cristiano Ronaldo has a strong passion for the football game. Cristiano's passion for his game is not questionable in any way, it has been shown on several occasions. We have seen him cry several times on the pitch. This great man cries when he loses a game he expects to win, he cries when he is unfairly suspended from a game he truly wants to play, he cries when he loses a final. In fact, the most remarkable show of intense emotion that still speaks volumes about his passion for his game was his reaction when he was injured from the hard tackle given to him by the French man, Payet in the final of Euro tournament of the year, 2016.

On the realization that he could no longer continue the game, he cried on the pitch before he was carried out of the field of play. His passion for the game never made him sit down to endure the pain of the injury he sustained, he went on to take up the role of a manager to cheer up and motivate his teammates

Flavours of a sweet rivalry

and he succeeded in cheering his team to victory. The secret of success in whatever you do is just to develop passion for what you do and nurture the passion.

Ronaldo's passion can also be seen in finals. After each final, one out of two things certainly happens. It is either he sheds tears of joy or he cries for his loss. Now do you think that a person who has such an emotion for his game would trivialize his game in any way?

What are the inferences?
You need sufficient energy to continue doing what you are doing, and this energy is supplied by passion. When you are passionate about what you do, the drive to keep doing what you do would increase in you. Your passion for what you do can rightly be likened to the chemical fuel that moves vehicles. Without the fuel, vehicles cannot successfully move. The passion triggers the secretion of some chemical fluids in you which give you the ability to keep going. These fluids include dopamine and adrenaline. The latter gives you more and more energy, while the former intensifies your passion for what you do.

Passion gives you a reason to carry on. This is absolutely true, as you wouldn't be doing something your heart is not fully into. As long as your heart is fully into what you do, you will always find reasons to carry on. Let's draw an inference from an illustration using marriage. What binds a man and a woman to remain knotted together until death separates them is simply Love. This love can be created by several factors such as physical looks of any of the couples, mannerisms of any of the couples, children that come into the family. Whatever is creating the love, the love is the major factor that keeps the couple together for a very long time. In the same vein when you develop love or passion for whatever you do, the passion would create in you commitment and this commitment makes you stick around for a long time. And the longer you stay, the more you improve in the field, acquiring more skills and getting better until you become the best at what you do.

Cristiano Ronaldo's commitment to the game is incomparable. Some of his teammates attest to the fact that he is always the first to come for practice and the last to leave the training ground. Now, tell me "what else could propel such dedication in a man if not for passion for what he does." Well, his commitment to his game is one of the reasons why he is arguably the best player in the game.

So, to be the best in your own world or field, allow the

passion to grow in you and allow it to give birth in you, dedication and commitment, that way, you would be the very best.

Ronaldo felt unhappy when he was confined for a long time in an isolated place as a result of testing positive for Covid-19. At some point of his confinement, he expressed his frustration through his social media handle. He mentioned that the isolation was getting longer than normal, perhaps he was missing the smell of the green grass in the football pitch.

Ronaldo also feels frustrated when he is not scoring or when he is substituted for another player in the middle of a game. All these are manifestations of his passion for the game. And these are reasons why he remains at the top.

Bottom line is that if you want to remain at the top of your game, have sufficient passion for your game.

Flavours of a sweet rivalry

MAGIC WAND OF MESSI

The Messi who shows no mercy
Who demolishes all, even Chelsea
Though pretty but he has no pity
His mercilessness gives us beauty

His works almost coated with lucks
His stars always graces his walks
His moves accurate like clockwork
His intricacies come with accuracy
The magic wand of Lionel Messi

Whatever that touches his feet
Simply turns into a beautiful gold
His footballing arts, wits and feat
Give us sweet memories to hold

Scoring from unimaginable angles
That sounds like what magicians do
Pulling out dribbles so impossible
Nice gifts he offers to me and you

He runs with others this soccer race
But it seems he runs with grace
He does with ease what seems hectic
His works are like film tricks and magics

His plays are almost coated with luck

Flavours of a sweet rivalry

> He has the keys to open every lock
> Are the intrigues by grace or by luck?
> Give it out to the Magician Messi
> Accurate master of magical intricacies

The Flavour
Some people believe in the concept of luck while others don't really believe in luck, they hold onto the belief that luck happens when an opportunity meets an adequate preparation.

So for a person to be successful, he has to adequately prepare for success. Now when an opportunity surfaces, and this person is able to utilize this opportunity, the preparation that has already been made would make the person achieve his goals. That is one of the ways people get lucky.

Now the question is; Are there people who are naturally more lucky than others?
The answer may be Yes. However it is important to point out that these individuals may also be endowed with more special abilities. But what makes them stand out is the fact that they are always prepared to grab opportunities. Preparation is very important to the achievement of success. And Lionel Messi is one the players who places a premium on preparation. Other players do place a premium on preparation, but are they as gifted as Lionel Messi? I doubt it.

Some football fans hold onto a view that Cristiano Ronaldo works harder than Lionel Messi, in the sense that Ronaldo arrives very early for practice and leaves very late. And of course, Ronaldo shows off some of his training sessions on social media. Well, the fact that Messi does not show us all his training sessions does not mean that he does not work hard enough. His accuracy on the field of play can only be a product of diligent, consistent hard work.

Now, I would like to introduce to you a unique kind of preparation, which takes place in the mind. Anybody who is great in what he does, thinks about what he does on a regular basis. The activities of what he does are always in his thoughts, they are in his sleeping thoughts and in his waking thoughts. I am sure that players like Messi and Ronaldo think about football, eat football and live football. And no other form of preparation beats this kind. This is because they have practically made football an integral part of their lives.

What are the inferences?
No beautiful performance is produced by luck alone. Always create a room for adequate preparation. In whatever you do, ensure that you fortify yourself with adequate preparation and practice before

stepping up to perform. If you are a teacher, ensure that you arm yourself with sufficient knowledge about your subject matter before you teach. If you are a performer, say a singer, dancer, spoken word artist, etc., ensure that you have proper rehearsals behind the stage before stepping up to perform. The truth of the matter is that the actual work takes place behind the stage. A stage performance should merely be an activity used to showcase what has already been completed. Every dirty game has already been completed behind the stage.

If you are into a trade, your preparation comes in the form of raising all required resources prior to the business. These resources may be capital, labor force, a site for the business and so on. These things should be procured before the commencement of the business. When all these are put in place, then it can be said that you have adequately prepared. Now if you are able to grab the opportunity to offer the needs of people to them in your environment, that would tantamount to opportunity meeting preparation, and that would consequently make you lucky in that business.

As a student too, before you step into an Examination hall, you must prepare the same way Messi and Ronaldo prepare for big games. You must prepare both in your mind and outside your mind. You must read and fortify yourself with knowledge. Now when you are opportune to encounter what you have read in the Examination hall, then luck will play out for you and you will excel.

Flavours of a sweet rivalry

THE DETERMINATION OF RONALDO

The letter C is for Cristiano
The letter R is for Ronaldo
The letter C is for commitment
The letter R is for Resilience
The number 7 is for perfection
Perfectly consistent is Ronaldo

When the odds are against
He never says Never
He is a true believer
That the next shall be the best

When he tries and falls
He rises to try again
He dares to give his all
Enduring all the pain

When his lucky stars seem so dim
He believes they can shine
He holds on to his mind's dream
For his gifts are divine

He who fights and runs today
Comes back to fight another day
Give it out to Cristiano the fighter
If Lionel is is a Lion, then he's a Tiger

Flavours of a sweet rivalry

The Flavour

It would be difficult to be absolutely successful by starting, stopping, and starting again. No, success does not come that way. What brings about success are persistence, commitment and consistency. And these qualities are found in Mr. Cristiano Ronaldo as well as in Mr. Lionel Messi. These amazing players are consistent in what they do. When you watch their styles of play, you would still observe that they still apply the same techniques that have brought them success over the years. And they hardly relinquish in the face of opposition.

It took Ronaldo several years of trials and errors to at last help his national team to lift an international trophy in the year 2016. An individual who is not that success hungry may give up when his hard work does not yield the expected result after several attempts but Cristiano never gave up. He kept on trying until he won something for his country, Portugal. In fact Portugal also went on to win another trophy a couple of years after.

Ronaldo's determination was also seen in his attempt to score a perfect bicycle kick goal. His "Never saying Never quality" paid off in 2018 on that champions league night where Juventus played against Real Madrid. His bicycle kick goal was so perfect and

Flavours of a sweet rivalry

beautiful that the fans of Juventus, his opposition as at that point in time, gave him a standing ovation. But the question is; "Do we know how many failed attempts of bicycle kick goals he had prior to that very night?" But did he ever stop trying to score? The answer is No. He kept on trying until his determination to score that desired goal came true. In fact, that particular goal against Juventus has been named the best goal in the history of the UEFA champions league (though it is likely to be argued), but Show me a better goal than that in the history of Champions league.

One spectacular thing that makes Cristiano Ronaldo exceptional is his quality of remaining persistent and consistent in the pursuance of his goals.

What are the inferences?

The lessons to be learnt from the determination is simply that we should not quit because we fail or because we feel tired. We should keep on pressing until the goal is achieved. The goal should be to achieve the goal. Anything other than that should not affect the process or the hard work in any way. In fact, the fact that you are failing in the process to achieve the goal should give you more and more reasons to work even harder. Until the goal is achieved.

Flavours of a sweet rivalry

The number of times you tried and failed does not really matter. What people remember in the future is that you eventually got it right. Nobody remembers those failed attempts of Cristiano Ronaldo to score a bicycle kick goal, but the picture of the beautiful bicycle kick goal that he eventually scored against Juventus will remain indelible in the hearts of all football fans. So as long as you know and understand what you are chasing after, stay focused and determine in your mind that you would never be at ease until your desires are achieved.

Those who start and stop always end up as failures, they hardly go too far. The reign of Ronaldo and Messi for more than a decade cannot be a function of some sort of luck, it is rather a function of diligent consistency and commitment. People who lack determination can neither be committed nor consistent.

If you have any strategy that works for you, stay true to it. Don't jump from one boat to another. As long as that strategy has once worked for you, when you always apply the same strategy, it will always work for you and if it always works for you, the best thing is to just stick to it. As you keep on getting good results from the strategy, you will tend towards being successful at what you do.

DETERMINATION OF MESSI

Taking on ten players to score
Passing to no one at all
Can only be done by an entity
Who feeds on risks and stays healthy

Losing out in a couple of finals
And hoping to someday clinch the cup
Can only be seen in Ronaldo's rival
The consistent Messi who never drops

Losing in several finals
But saying it is not the final
Can only be seen in a determined mind
Who hustles until honours, he finds

Running, staggering but never falling
Though being dragged by a million hands
Falling eventually and quickly rising
Never staying forever on the sands
Can only be seen in a determined man
Messi plays as one who has a plan

Winning a million golden boots
Winning a billion Ballon d'or
Winning daily and seeking for more
Can only be achieved

Flavours of a sweet rivalry

By a man with a magical left foot

The Flavour

It only takes a very determined mind to lose in more than three finals after seasons of hard work, to remain focused and still play with the same energy, if not more energy. This is the case of Lionel Messi. Prior to 2016, Messi had lost in a couple of finals which included a World cup final. And the pathetic part of it is that he always gave his best to those tournaments in which he was losing in the finals. This is evident in the fact that he was named the best player of most of those tournaments. In reality, for an average player, it is easy to relinquish everything after making those frantic efforts to win at least a trophy for his country and his efforts always hit the rocks. In fact, his frustration was obvious when he lost the Copa America trophy to Chile in the year 2016 in a penalty shoot out. After that loss, he announced his retirement from international football. That sounds like giving up, right? But it was actually due to his passion for the game and hunger to win.

Being a very determined person, when he was begged to reconsider his stance, he didn't blink, he rejoined his national team and the struggles continued. He devoted more hard work to win something for the team. Now the question is; "Did the hard work later

Flavours of a sweet rivalry

pay off? Of Course the hard work did pay off. Hard work never goes unrewarded. Just like Ronaldo, he has so far helped his national team, Argentina to win two international trophies. And he will be among the Argentina squad who will be playing in the 2022 World cup in Qatar (This book was published a month before the Qatar 2022 World cup).

Determination is also seen in Messi's style of play. Show me another player who can have the courage to dribble up to six players at a time. Messi takes on multiple players, runs through any space he sees, dribbles them and sometimes, still scores. It takes courage and determination to do that. He has the mindset of wanting to see what happens if he does not give up. Hence he does not bother about passing the ball to his teammates. He goes on to do everything and at last, he still scores.

What are the Inferences?

Nothing good comes that easily. Every good achievement is obtained through some diligent determination. Whatever it is that your heart desires, you have to believe that you can achieve it. And you have to allow this belief to create in you, the determination to achieve.

Determination fills you up with sufficient energy

Flavours of a sweet rivalry

which can make you relentless. When you are relentless, the only thing that makes you stop trying is when you have achieved your goal.

As a success minded individual, you must be able to set goals and you must be determined enough to accomplish those goals, regardless of what it can take from you.

Determination keeps you focused on your goals. Do you see how focused Messi appears to be whenever he is determined to score a goal? That spirit of success that always comes to take over his determined mind whenever he is about to score, makes him focus on the ball and at the goal post.

Determination also gives you trackways to follow in order to achieve your goals. When you see Messi dribbling multiple players, it is because of the kind of mind he carries. The determined kind of mind that he carries is what shows him the ways to move as he dribbles those family men on the pitch of play.

The same also applies to you in real life. When your mind and heart are determined to achieve a definite feat, the pathways to easily achieve that feat would easily be revealed to you.

In all your gettings, get the determination of Lionel Messi.

Flavours of a sweet rivalry

HARD WORK OF RONALDO

He shows up in the pitch
When mates are still in bed
Stretches to all heights' reach
Give it out to the early bird
He stays in the pitch
When mates have gone to bed
Little wonder he is rich
By greatness he is fed

The skills he lack, he desires
And;
By stretching his back, he acquires
He never says Nay in the face
of an opposition, all challenges
He heartily embraces

His muscles are fed with energy
To chase after all records
So reckless he is with records
Today he is breaking them
Morrow, he is creating them
He never on his way acquires lethargy

Give it out to the go-getter
King Ronaldo the dreams chaser
Give it out to the hard worker

Flavours of a sweet rivalry

> King Cristiano the game changer
> Whatever he touches simply glitters
> Even more than gold shines brighter

The Flavour

Energy and drive are vital to the achievement of success in any field. Sufficient energy and drive give you reasons to carry on. And guess who is so energetic as a Lion? Your guess is absolutely right. Ronaldo!.

Show me another player who works as hard as Cristiano Ronaldo. In one of his responses to interview questions, Dr. Sir Alex Ferguson, a one time manager of Cristiano Ronaldo mentioned that Ronaldo was always the first to arrive at the training ground and the last to leave, now tell me how possible it would be for such a player to play at the same level as other players?

We have been made to understand that the beauty of a performance is dependent on the quality of preparation a person makes. Being devoted to practice and training can actually make a person stand out among his equals. Now the question is; "From where does Cristiano draw this level of energy?" The answer is simple. This unimaginable energy of Cristiano Ronaldo comes from two main sources, namely:

- Desires to achieve and win
- Passion for the game

Desire to win: Having a strong desire can be a driving force that can push a person to want to win. In one of the interviews that Cristiano granted, when he was asked about why he gets frustrated when he loses, he simply replied, "because I love to win" and it is that simple. He sees himself as a born winner. And this perception he has about himself makes him have that strong desire to always win. And for him to always accomplish his desire, there has to be sufficient energy. This is why he does some unimaginable things, such as running with a great speed, and jumping as though gravity has no effect on him, even at his age, among other extraordinary things he does.

Passion for the game: Passion is another reason why Cristiano Ronaldo shows unimaginable energy and drive in his game. It is not questionable that Cristiano loves the game of football. I can vividly remember how his countenance was the first time he was substituted in Real Madrid, he obviously was not happy with Coach Zinedine Zidane for truncating his playing time. That attribute can only be seen in a man who is passionate about his game. Now if he would feel that bad for being substituted, that means that he would always like to play for an entire 90 minutes duration. And for this reason, he would want to give his very best so that the manager would not see a reason to want to replace him. And giving out the best in this case requires energy and hard work. Now I believe that it is clear to see where he draws his energy from.

What are the inferences?
You must develop a strong passion for whatever you do. For passion supplies you the fuel you need to keep moving and growing.

You must also desire to be great in what you do and you must vehemently shun laziness and lethargy. You must not always sit down saying that you are tired of doing something, for that would be the enemy of your progress in life. You must as well stop giving excuses as regards why you cannot do what you are supposed to do. You must always get up to do what you have to do everyday. You must vehemently shun procrastination.

Procrastination is an enemy of success. People who procrastinate always end up at the average level, they are never as exceptional as Cristiano. If Cristiano always procrastinates as to what time he should start practice, do you think he would be this good?

You just need to work with the mindset that "whatever is worth doing, is worth doing well." And if it is actually worth doing well, you should love it and invest your maximum energy in doing it.

FOCUS OF MESSI

Eyes on the goal
Shoes on the sole
Feet take control
of the spherical ball

Eyes on the net
Feet truly set
the ball in motion
Creating commotion

Free kicks like clock work
Hat tricks not by lucks
Locks to records he unlocks
Keys to records he uses to lock

His ears are deaf to noise
His eyes fixed on his choice
He hears his mind's voice
And by it, he stays focused

Eyes on the goal
He dares to win the whole
He knows well his roles
He dares to take control
of the spherical ball
Messi, the king over all

Flavours of a sweet rivalry

When he's with the ball
He runs to his destination
Tho, he's pushed to fall
But he stays true to his focus

He focuses on his focus
And of course he scores
His eyes are on the goal
That's why he takes control

The Flavour

Every successful person is a focused person. His or her eye is only on the goal. Other things may not be of importance to him or her. Every effort he makes is geared towards achieving that big goal. If you watch Lionel Messi, you would understand that he is a man of vision and focus. If you watch him taking on players (with his speed, twists, turns and dribbles), if you see him take a free kick or if you see him give a long pass to a teammate, you will be able to recognize that he is a man of focus and vision.

In most cases, when he runs to score with the ball, several players try to stop him by pushing and pulling him. But does that stop him? No, it does not stop him in any way. When he plays a free kick, the motion of the ball and the direction that it takes to get to the back of the net tells you that the calculation of those angles has already been made by a focused mind.

Now, let's come out a little bit, Players as good as Messi and Ronaldo, regardless of how good they are, still get trolls who sometimes disparage and boo them. They get negative comments from the foes of their fans. But do those things affect their game? The answer is No. This is simply because they are focused on what they do.

Messi and Ronaldo are likely to always set out a definite number of goals they intend to score every season. And the only way to achieve their set out goals is by staying focused on the goals.

What are the inferences?
No good success can be achieved by an easily distracted person. Your focus should always be on your goal. In your field, you should always focus on achieving the best feat. Move towards achieving your goals everyday and let nothing stop you.

You must learn how to not let oppositions and challenges stop you. Yes, as long as you are doing something meaningful, you must face challenges. But what makes your success beautiful is your ability to

Flavours of a sweet rivalry

win despite all life's challenges.

Just like Lionel Messi, Refuse to give up when oppositions try to pull or push you down. Stand firm and fight like a Lion, the same way Lionel fights to overcome his challenges and win like the Lion he is.
Don't be stopped by fears. Learn to drain your fear. Always take the risk, if you fall, you would be wiser and if you triumph, you would be happy. Taking on up to 5 or 6 players, dribbling them while their family members watch, and daring to score afterwards must be a very big risk. However Messi takes the risk without fear. And it has paid off a couple of times. This is one of the reasons he is seen as a magician.
So learn to drain your fear. Take a bold step and take that big step. Invest that money, start up that project, start writing that book, start that training right now. Whatever you intend to do, start doing it right now and stay focused on it. It will surely be rewarding.

Flavours of a sweet rivalry

THE RESILIENCE OF RONALDO

He's not a bouncing baby boy
But he bounces back like a spring
Under pressure he sometimes coils
But he is still the lord of the ring
Glory to his team he always brings

When the pressure is so tensed
Pressure without measure
He is fed with immeasurable vigor
He thrives in the ring though in pains

He is like a cat with nine lives
He takes a break from today's fight
So that he can fight tomorrow
And tomorrow he shows up in might
Breaking the hearts of men and wives
Causing the fans pleasurable sorrow

The number of times he falls
Is not important as long as
He can get as much goal calls
And beautiful assisting pass
From teammates just to score

He is not by pressure, suppressed
Whenever he feels compressed

Flavours of a sweet rivalry

> Like a compressed spring
> He bounces back again
> He's the lord of his ring
> He has an eternal reign

The Flavour

"Success is sweet but life is not a bed of roses." For every successful person who has lived on this earth or who still lives on this earth, there are always rocky experiences. Successful people never have it easy.

The case of Thomas Edison who had over ninety failed attempts in the course of trying to create a working electric bulb is a typical example. Some other inventors also had their fair shares of trying and failing until they came up with something they could show off. In fact, we are not unfamiliar with the stories of some politicians who contest for a political position a number of times until they eventually get lucky at a lucky single time. Well, the number of times a person falls in his quest to achieve greatness does not really count. What matters is his ability to rise again and try again each time he falls.

The case of Cristiano Ronaldo is not quite an exception, in his career, he has had his fair share of trying and failing. But does that keep him down? The answer is No. He is resilient. He bounces back after each downfall.

On multiple occasions, Cristiano Ronaldo has been the player to overturn the score in cases where his team was losing. This quality made him become Diego Simeone's nightmare. He deprived Simeone the privilege of winning the champions league. Then, It was always a case of Diego Simeone's Atletico Madrid's side taking the lead either in the first half of a game or in the first leg of an encounter between Ronaldo's side and Diego's side. On multiple occasions, Cristiano Ronaldo always brought heartbreak to Diego Simeone, the manager of Atletico, bouncing back from hopelessness to win the game.

His resilience in the aspect of his rivalry with Messi in terms of winning the Ballon d'or award has been over stressed. At a point when he had only one Ballon d'or, Messi had four. But Ronaldo was resilient enough to catch up with Messi so that at a particular point in 2017, he had the same number of Ballon d'or as Lionel Messi (they were tied at 5 Ballon d'or for each of them).

Cristiano has also restored hope to his team when they seem to play below the average level. Check out what he does in Portugal.

What are the inferences?

Don't remain down when you fall down. When you fall, pick yourself back up and try again. Be determined to succeed and your determination would make you resilient. When you make a mistake, don't allow your mistake to cause you to appear as a mistake. You are only human and you are bound to be imperfect. What matters is that your eye is on the goal. When you decide to rise from your mistakes and try again, you do better on the next attempt, this is because there are a number of things you would learn from your mistake. And there are things you would not like to repeat so that you don't make the same mistake twice.

In summary, don't be a person who cracks under pressure. Let the pressure be the push that you need to prove that you are good at what you do. One of the things that make Ronaldo stand out is that he is able to deliver to the fullest even when he is under pressure. That is called "Resilience".

You need to be resilient in your endeavors too. As life's challenges try to beat you into shapes, determine for yourself the shape you want to assume.

Flavours of a sweet rivalry

THE ACCURACY OF MESSI

When he starts a race
With the ball in his feet
He never stops
He continues in his pace
Until all opponents retreat
And the ball in the post drops

When he freely kicks
The ball from every distance
His vision is focused on a dot
And on the dot he aims his kick
The ball moves in obedience
To the direction of his shot

When he gets a through pass
From a mate
But he is determined to score
He never gives back the pass
To any other mate
He dangles around until he scores

He rarely jumps but when he jumps
His head goes higher and higher
To a point that he touches the ball
And this touch makes a pump
A pump to push the ball further

Flavours of a sweet rivalry

Further behind the goalie's all

Lionel Andres Messi
The Lion who shows no Mercy
Master in magical consistency
The Messi who knows no mercy
He's a Master in precise accuracy

The Flavour

Messi believes that it is better to get it right at the very first attempt than to keep trying and trying. He believes that when he gets it right at the very first attempt, there would be no need to keep trying over and over again. This precious belief that he has makes him to apply diligence and precision in what he does.

Whenever he is with the ball, he is almost excellent with the ball, everything he does with the ball is close to perfect. When he takes a free kick, he carefully plans for it before he kicks and this plan brings about precision. When you see him dribble, he displays some excellent moves. The ball gets stuck to his feet as though it is glued to his feet. Every move he makes is perfect. He believes that it is best to get it right the very first time than to be struggling over and again.

When it comes to football, you cannot mention the

word, "Precision" without thinking about Lionel Messi. You also cannot talk about accuracy without mentioning Lionel Messi. And these two qualities are very pivotal to the achievement of success. It is true that no human is perfect, however when a person is able to effectively and efficiently exhibit a high level of precision and accuracy, that person can be said to be close to perfection. Yes, Lionel Messi is not a perfect human being but when it comes to football, he is close to being perfect, the same can also be said about Cristiano Ronaldo.

What are the inferences?
Always make your first impression beautiful for it matters a whole lot. Always look out for accuracy and precision. Don't take things for granted no matter how small or insignificant they may seem to appear. Give your best to the small things because a number of small are the things that aggregate to form the big things. Nobody can easily dislike a beautiful work. And what makes your work beautiful are accuracy and precision.

The way you would prepare to display before a president or any other important personality, should be the same way you should prepare to display before a common individual. The energy you would exhibit when called out to a big stage should be the same energy you should showcase when you are called to perform on a small stage where the spectators are very few. Whatever you think is worth is worth doing with precision and accuracy.

Flavours of a sweet rivalry

HAUGHTY HUMILITY OF RONALDO

Yes, he is haughty
But with a good motive
He is not as haughty
As Ibrahimovic'
Not as humble
As Lionel Messi
He is just Ronaldo

Yes he can brag
But after his bragging
Several honours he bags
Hmm... Goals are banging

After his wonder and drama
And he gets no good plaudits
While teammates get the credits
He displays some melodrama
He's not as humble as Sadio
He is just Cristiano Ronaldo

He is very haughty
When you view from afar
But he feeds on humility
And drinks from humility jar
Not as humble as Salah Mo'
He is just Cristiano Ronaldo

Jealousy makes him haughty
He wants to get it all
This also gives him his beauty
As he stands very tall
Not as haughty as Neymar
Not as humble as Neymar
He is just a unique star

Haughtily humble maybe
Well, he shows his true self
Maybe, He's humbly haughty
He doesn't hide in a cave

MAY C.Ronaldo be as humble
As Lionel MESSI
But Cristiano can only be Ronaldo
And Lionel can only be Messi

The Flavour

From the above poem, a perceived negative part of Cristiano Ronaldo is pointed out. This perceived negative part is haughtiness. Only a small number of football fans would agree that Ronaldo is humble. But the truth is that he truly is, for it would be so difficult for a person who has no element of humility to remain at that top level for years.

Flavours of a sweet rivalry

Cristiano Ronaldo is just jealous of his name. Yes he tries at all costs to perform up to his big name. He sees his name as one of the biggest names in football, little wonder why the number 7 jersey number is attributed to him,m. Every club he plays in, reserves the number 7 jersey for him. The humility of Ronaldo is referred to as a haughty humility.

It is true that pride goes before a fall, but a little bit of pride coated with humility is important for one to succeed in life. It may be important to sometimes show off and talk about your achievements but remember not to allow the beautiful achievements to get into your head.

The reason why you should be haughtily humble is simply to make it clear that you are at the top level. And once you are aware of the fact that people see you at a top level, you will be so conscious not to embarrass yourself with a below average performance.

This element of haughty humility is shown by every great person directly or indirectly. It is the flavour needed to retain the very top spot. Even Lionel Messi who appears to be humble to the core also has this haughty humility. His haughty humility may not be that evident as that of Cristiano because he is

Flavours of a sweet rivalry

relatively more shy than Cristiano.

The haughty humility of Messi is always displayed but his shy nature still makes all see him as humble. An instance of Messi's haughty humility was in the el-classico game where he scored that winning goal with which Barcelona got a 3-2 victory over their arch rival, Real Madrid. To celebrate the goal, he took out his shirt and displayed his name and number at the back of the shirt to the fans of Real Madrid. Wow!!! **The humble Messi?**

Well, that's what we mean by haughty humility. That singular act would definitely make him put more effort into improving in his game, because after showing off such a display, fumbling in the next game would only bring embarrassment. So in a bid to avoid any form of embarrassment, he would give his best in every next game. Yes this is true. In fact to consolidate this fact, we can remember that in the next season when Ronaldo scored Barcelona in a classico game, he replicated that Messi's celebration, yes he also showed the Barcelona fans his own name and jersey number. Now, that would have been very embarrassing to Messi if he wasn't playing at a top level.

So speaking about or advertising your good work isn't

bad at all. It is what you need to grow in your field. It is what would make the people know you better. And exposure is simply what you need to be at the top level.

After winning his first Ballon d'or, Ronaldo vowed that he would win the award again. Hmm....That might not sound humble, but it turned everyone's focus on him. And he understood that he had to play up to the braggings to avoid embarrassment. And of course he did play up to the bragging and he went on to win four extra Ballon d'or awards.

What are the inferences?
Learn how to market yourself, learn how to advertise your craft. At the end of the day, life is all about what you make from it.

Don't let your humility keep you in obscurity, show forth your good works. Speak of your achievements in a way that your speaking spurs you to want to achieve more. Speak of your achievements in a way that you inspire other people to want to achieve what you have achieved. Do not hide your abilities, make them believe that you are able to do it.

However while you show off your beauty, don't do it in a completely haughty way, rather do it in a

Flavours of a sweet rivalry

haughtily humble way.

The bottom line is this; Do not be too humble that your brilliance is masked by your humility. Show yourself off, but do it in a humble way. Have the belief that you are better than the rest, you can vocalize it like Cristiano does or act it like Messi does. But always remember to show respect to everyone.

Flavours of a sweet rivalry

THE HUMILITY OF MESSI

Where is Messi in the photograph?
I mean the team photograph
He's somewhere at the back
But why does he stay that far?
I'm sure he scored the winner
The showy attitude he lacks

Though arguably the best
He offers himself no praise
He still takes the same place
Which is taken by the rest

Yea he deserves all the glory
But he shies away from plaudits
His humility writes his story
He gives to others the credits

He has reasons to be haughty
His cabinets are filled with trophies
His playing art keeps men frozen
But his honours make him not naughty
For he feeds on the meat of modesty

Though he sits on the kingdom's throne
The soccer kingdom throne
Whenever he scores a goal
His hand and eyes up they go

Flavours of a sweet rivalry

To show he has no power of his own
He still rever the mighty one above
His humility earns him my pen's love

The Flavour
One special and heavenly attribute in Lionel Messi is his humility. This attribute endears him to many people including my pen. Though he is always the best player in every team he plays in, he does not lord over his teammates. He does not see himself standing on the same level as his achievements. Whenever he speaks of himself, he never gives himself inordinate praises. Whenever he wins an individual award, he gives credits to his teammates and manager (Cristiano also does that same). He never takes all the glory to himself.

In fact the iconic, Lionel Messi's celebration of raising two hands up while looking up whenever he scores a goals is another mark of humility as he gives God the glory perhaps for blessing him with all the beautiful footballing skills that he has, even though speculations have it that the celebration is a way of dedicating his goals to his late grandmother who supported his game in the early stage of his career. However my pen still believes that the celebration is a symbol of his humility.

Whenever his team wins a trophy or an important

game, even though he is the player that saves the day, you would never see him flashing his face to the camera to be seen by all. You would rather see him in the background as the team takes a photograph.

What are the inferences?
We shall draw our inferences from the popular saying, "Pride goes before a fall." Most people who have allowed pride to have the better part of them easily stumble on the way. Pride is the major factor that brings complacency and self-satisfaction and like we have stressed, Complacency is one of the major reasons people remain on the average level.

One thing about being prideful is that, when you are prideful, you automatically make people have a very high expectation of you, because you unconsciously send a message to them that you can operate on a level higher than the one you are currently operating. Now, when you fail to put in sufficient hard work to operate on that high level which you have placed yourself, you might be doing well, but the people who now have high expectations of you would not appreciate what you do. And they will consequently see you as a failure or a person who operates at just the average level.

Now, on the other hand, when you are very humble, people will not have high expectations of you, thereby

Flavours of a sweet rivalry

making every simple thing you do to be well appreciated. And when you are appreciated for the simple things you do, you would have chances to grow. Because even when you are not performing very well, nobody condemns or attacks you because you never gave them any impression that you will always show greatness.

Humility attracts people's love and support. Yes, this is true, people are naturally attracted to other persons who they perceive to be humble. And when this love is created, it becomes very easy for the humble to be helped.

In your journey through life's path, you need the help of other individuals to get to the pinnacle of your success ladder. As you cannot be an island of your own. Now, if you are haughty, arrogant and proud, you would rather repel people more than you would attract them. And when people are repelled by your haughtiness, it would become difficult for them to give you support when you are in need of it.

Humility makes you approachable. Yes again, people tend to speak with you freely when they perceive that you are humble. Now, it may interest you to know that most people who succeeded in their respective fields succeeded because they made good use of

Flavours of a sweet rivalry

opportunities that came at some point in time. Now, assuming you are very haughty and arrogant, if an opportunity that you know not about comes up in your field, will your colleagues be free enough to approach and speak to you about the opportunity or will they be repelled by your haughtiness? Think about it.

Humility is one of the priceless virtues. Most football fans, especially the fans of Cristiano Ronaldo, accuse Messi of being favoured by FIFA and UEFA ahead of Ronaldo. Well, I don't know whether the speculations are true or not, but if they are true, it may be because one of the players seems to be more humble than the other.

The bottom line is that humility will help you way more than pride will ever help you.

Flavours of a sweet rivalry

THE WONDERS OF RONALDO

When his feet fly so high
He never on the ground drops
Until his head to the ball says Hi
And the ball in the post stops

When he freely kicks
the ball, from the spot of penalty
The goalie serves the penalty
For daring to spoil his trick
He kicks with accuracy
Forming several angles of 90

When the ball embraces his feet
And he recalls that he is selfish
He runs in from all inches and feets
He stops not until his run is polished
Polished by the ball behind the goalie
Polished by his beautiful accuracy

When his left foot or right strikes
The goal post and goalie tremble
Tremble to be hit by a power bike
However they take the pain not to fumble

When his back heels act
Their actions know more accuracy
Than the front foot of most soccer arts

Flavours of a sweet rivalry

He gives the football game much beauty

The Flavour
Whatever it is that's worth doing, is worth doing well. Cristiano Ronaldo knows this fact. This is why he tries to add beauty to everything he does. He tries to make himself unique in everything. He has his unique style of play. He has his unique ways of scoring. He even has his trademark celebration which is known to belong to just him. Is that not wonderful? This touch of uniqueness makes him stand out in everything.

Show me another player that does leg over and is uniquely known for doing leg over, Show me another player that stands the way he stands prior to taking a free kick or a penalty kick. Show me another player who jumps as high as he does in order to score a beautiful header. Show me another player who has a trademark celebration that's as famous as Cristiano's "Siuuu Celebration".

Well the above mentioned unique qualities of Cristiano are what make him stand out from the crowd. In my clime, those unique qualities are parts of what we call "packaging and branding". Good packaging and branding are important in business. You have to be known for something unique and beautiful.

What are the inferences?
You need to carve a niche for yourself and be known for something. And you need to add uniqueness to that thing you are known for. To whatever you do, Add a touch of uniqueness. This is simply because of the fact that you cannot be the first person to have ever belonged to that field, but you can be the first person to have ever done the things you do in the very unique ways you do them.

Cristiano is not the only player that uses those football skills, but for the fact that those skills are used in Cristiano's way, that makes him stand out. So in whatever you do, dare to do it in a way that nobody has ever done it. that would make you stand out.

If you are a writer, be a writer with a difference. Use writing skills that can make your writings irresistible. Are you a singer? Sing in a way that nobody has ever sung before. Add spicy flavours to your song, use angelic voice to sing if you can, make yourself irresistible. Are you a business person? Dare to make your trade stand out. Sell good products at unbeatable prices, offer good customer services and do good advertisements. As a student, give your very best to your studies, read to learn as though your life is dependent on your studies.

Always have a brand and strive to package your brand. The clothes sold in an average clothing store in the market may be the same as the one sold in a boutique, but what makes the ones sold in a boutique stand out is packaging. The rice sold in a local restaurant and the one sold in a high class restaurant both supply carbohydrates, but why do they have a difference in their prices? The answer is simple. The one sold in a high class restaurant has better packaging than the one sold in a local restaurant.

Now, it is expected that you should get the point. You can only be successful in what you do by adding beauty to what you do.

Flavours of a sweet rivalry

DISCIPLINE

I am Cristiano Ronaldo
I love to eat Potatoes
I can buy a million potatoes
But I'd rather eat a tomato
So I don't be a fat Ronaldo

My name is Cristiano Ronaldo
I live in a very expensive flat
But you may see me lie on a mat
For I love to be a strong Ronaldo

My name is Lionel Messi
I can afford the costliest diet
But for foods, I show Mercy
For the Lion has to watch his weight

My name is Lionel Messi
I can afford the best Canteen
But my game seeks consistency
Oh! I have to stick to its routine

We're the greatest of all times
Yeah we may be in our prime
But we still keep to the time
Never keep them to wait
No we never arrive late

Yeah we seem to be perfect
But we never disrespect mates
We are disciplined to the core
We nicely respond to every call

The standards must be followed
To the rules we must adhere
We have to surely win tomorrow
That's why we must train today

The Flavour
Show me a disciplined man and I will show you a successful man. Success in every field is absolutely reliant on a strict discipline. An undisciplined person would either do more than expected or below expectations and at last, tend towards failure. You cannot speak of discipline without mentioning the names of Ronaldo and Messi. Discipline is what actually brought them to this lofty height.

These two amazing players show a high level of discipline. They show discipline in the way they eat. It should not come as a surprise that Messi and Ronaldo are the top two richest footballers and for this reason, they can be able to afford anything they intend to buy. But why are they not too fat? The answer is simple. "They are disciplined". They show a high level of discipline in the way they eat and of course in their lifestyles. It may not come as a surprise that there are some starchy and fatty foods that may be avoided by these two players so that they may always be in good shape. We call that discipline.

Discipline can also be seen in the lives of Messi and Ronaldo in the aspect of their training/practice. It should not come as a surprise that these two fantastic players may hardly miss or skip training sessions. It has been said that Ronaldo even arrives at the training ground before every other person and leaves after every other person has left. This is more than discipline. He has kept to this routine for several years. That is a high level of self discipline.

They also show discipline in their manners and conduct. Irrespective of their achievements, they remain humble and respectful. They respect all the rules. They maintain a cordial relationship with teammates and managers, they give humble appreciation speeches, each time they win their awards.

What are the inferences?
In everything you do, you need to be disciplined to the core. Your success is tied to discipline. Your discipline starts by keeping to all the rules and regulations that

guide the field you are into. Then you must also have your personal principles and you must adhere to the principles and allow them to guide you.

You must make yourself a person of integrity, who would ensure that he always keeps to his own part of every bargain. Don't ever be found wanting when a deal is broken. Ensure that you always pay your dues.

Your discipline should always be seen in the way you dress, for you are addressed by how you are dressed.

Your discipline should also be seen in your choice of words. Try to always Speak politely and respectfully to people.

Your discipline should also be seen in the ways you approach things and your mannerisms. Be civil in your every approach. And act with decency. Let everything you do be done with moderation, dare not to be a glutton, don't be talkative, and don't readily show indiscipline.

Flavours of a sweet rivalry

TEAM WORK

Your identity is neither gotten
From one man's dexterity
Nor the other man's creativity
It is rather truly gotten
From the beauty in your unity

Appreciating the beauty in unity
Makes you to know
That you can only do well
When you together dwell
Synergy makes you grow

To reclaim your glowing show
To take back your showy glow
You have to return to the vision
The vision isn't to bring division
It's rather to remain as a single whole

The mission was never a me-ssion
For a me-ssion brings failure emission
The mission is truly a we-ssion
By a we-ssion we shall always win
Yea! Together, forever, win we shall
Hence we have to the idea of "me" shun

The Flavour
Each time Ronaldo or Messi gives a speech after

winning an award, you must always hear them appreciate their teammates for their efforts in making them win. They don't do this for the sake of formality. They do this rather in recognition of the fact that without the collective efforts of the team, they can hardly amount to those very magnificent heights of glory.

Irrespective of how good Ronaldo or Messi is, if their teammates decide not to support them in the field of play, they can never be regarded as two of the best players that have ever graced the field of football. Messi and Ronaldo are two unselfish players, even though people wrongly accuse Ronaldo of selfishness (I wonder what they say about Messi's style of always wanting to score a solo goal). Regardless of the playing styles of these amazing footballs they still rely on their teammates to pull out the beauty that they pull out.

Check out the number of times they have assisted other players to score. Check out the number of times they have sacrificed penalty kicks and free kicks to other players so that those players can also have some goals to their credits. Messi easily gives out a penalty to other players, even in cases where he needs just a goal from the penalty kick to complete a hat trick.

All these attributes point to the fact that the two amazing footballers understand the importance of teamwork in the achievement of success. We all need us to succeed.

What are the inferences?
Nothing beats unity. All can be achieved when there is unity. Drawing from a story from the Holy Bible, when men gathered together to build a house that could get to the sky, God would have just ignored them, but their unity could not just be ignored. And it took God bringing among them disunity in order to frustrate their plans. This implies that if God had not gone further to put in their tongues, different languages, they might have achieved their aim of building a structure that could touch the sky. So, unity and teamwork are very essential in the achievement of success.

In your work in your field, you need to learn how to interact with other people, especially, the people who can help you grow in the field. They can be the people who are better than you or the people who are not better than you, but are hungry for success. Learn to tap from the knowledge of other people to better and improve yourself.

Flavours of a sweet rivalry

Do not be an island of your own. No man is an island. No one knows it all. Learn to exchange ideas, give out the ideas you have and obtain their own ideas, then add the obtained ideas to the ones you already have. This is how you grow and develop.

Just like Ronaldo and Messi, when you are helped by other individuals, never forget to acknowledge their good contributions to your success, irrespective of how insignificant they may appear. By doing so, they would see reasons to want to be of help next time.

This poem titled, "Team work" was actually inspired after the reunion of the Nigerian musical group, "P-Square". This group consists of identical twin brothers whose real names are Peter and Paul. These talented singers began their musical careers as a team (a group). And as expected, they made a very great impact in the music industry. In their prime, they were arguably the best musical group in Africa.

However, due to some disagreements that ensued in the course of their journeys, they decided to go solo.

Well, each of them to the best of his ability had a successful solo career. They produced some good sounding tunes, each of them had a large number of crowd gracing their respective concerts, their music videos enjoyed several millions of views on YouTube. But the question is; Was the P-Square glory still there? No, the glory began to depart oo...

At some point, the Igbo Nigerian twins got to realize the importance of teamwork. What did they do after the realization? Of course they reunited. And as they reunited, the glory that they once enjoyed began to return. As you read right now, the glory must have fully returned. This is the power of teamwork.

Ronaldo and Messi understand the strength in teamwork. This is why they don't toy with having good relationships with their teammates and their managers.

LOVE FOR HUMANITY

Men with hearts of gold
Their bounties they don't withhold
Yeah! they are bountifully blessed
Their Bounties also aid the helpless

Men of Mercy and Compassion
With hearts of absolute purity
For their love for humanity
They sincerely give to Charity
What a different display of beauty!

Men with hearts to give
It's better to give than to receive
Yeah they give to relieve
Little wonder they always achieve

Men of Mercy and Compassion
They go as far as making donation
Donation of their precious blood
To the ailing in need of blood
They're divinely sent from above
To humanity they show great love

Men with hearts of gold
Even on pitches, they don't withhold
Passes they gives out to assist

Flavours of a sweet rivalry

To be the solitary king they don't insist

Men with hearts of gold
They can't stand bold to behold
homeless kids who sleep on roads
Homes, they give to the homeless
Expecting nothing in return
But by their acts they remain blessed
They get God's blessings in return

Men with golden hearts to give
This golden principle, they believe;
"It's better to give than to receive"
Hence, they give what they receive
Yeah they give so as to relieve
other men of pains they receive
Oh! Little wonder Messi achieves
as much as what Ronaldo achieves

Flavours of a sweet rivalry

A NEVER ENDING DEBATE

Who is better than the other
Some say Messi is good
But Ronaldo is better
So talented is Messi's foot
But Ronaldo works harder

Some say Ronaldo owns an airline
"Cr7 airline" that takes him so high
To score goals that are awesome
He also has an awesome hair line
Of course he is more handsome

Some call Messi a magician
Who does the incredible
He can run through a population
Just by the aid of dribbles

Some call Messi;
"The Greatest of all time"
Some also insist;
Ronaldo was incomparable in his prime

Some call Ronaldo a great goal scorer
While;
Some call Messi a better playmaker
Well;

Flavours of a sweet rivalry

The two kings always bang stunners
This debate might get even hotter

Some call Ronaldo a great team leader
Who shows up when needed the most
Some call Messi a fair weather player
Who under pressure disappears like a ghost

Some call Messi better
For having more Ballon d'or
Some call Ronaldo better
For having more Dubai d'or

Some think Messi is the goat
For he has more European golden boots
Some think Ronaldo is the goat
For he owns the world golden boot
Yea! He has the most international goals

This debate will be never ending
Will be always open to adjournment
The final verdict will always be pending
Let's just enjoy the entertainment

Flavours of a sweet rivalry

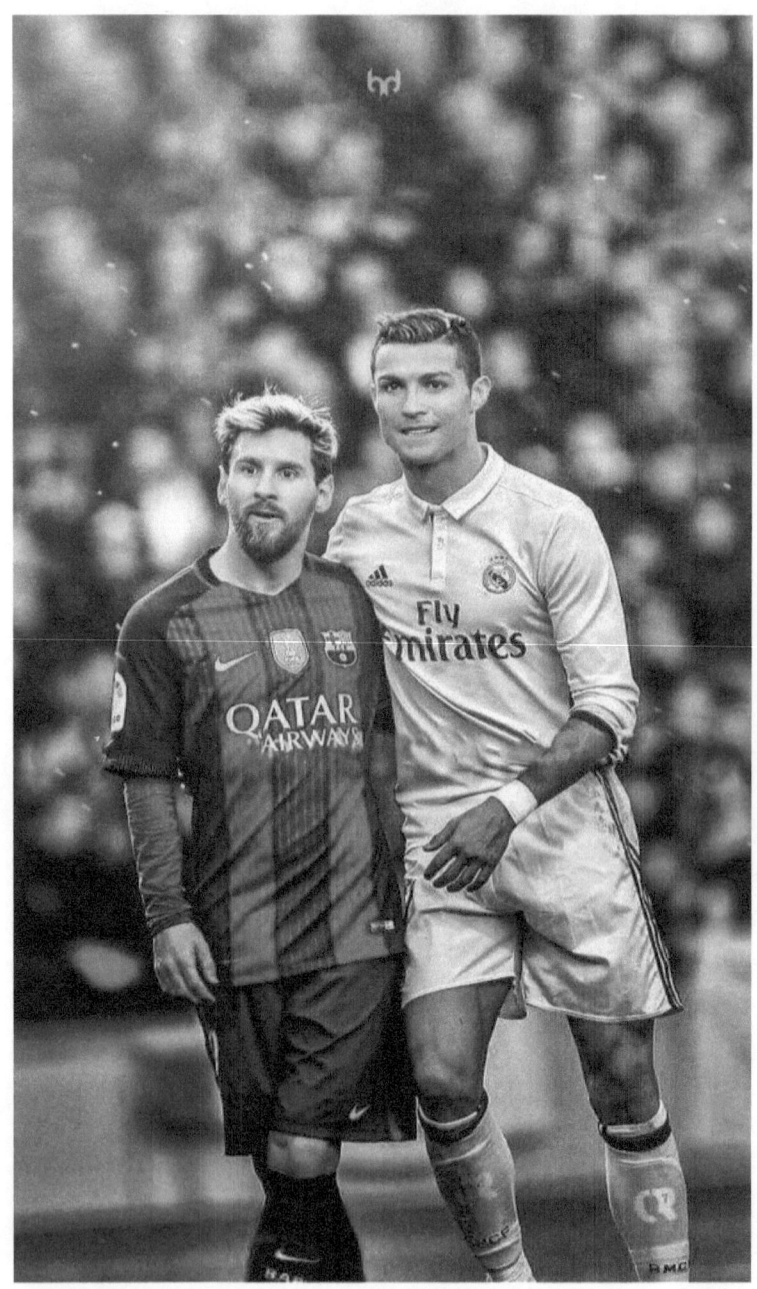